753 BC	The date when the Romans said Rome was founded
59 BC	Julius Caesar starts his wars in Gaul (France)
55/54 BC	Caesar invades Britain because he says the British are helping the Gauls
30 BC	Rome becomes the Roman Empire instead of the Roman Republic. Augustus becomes the first Emperor of Rome
AD 1	Traditional date for the birth of Jesus (in Israel, part of the Roman Empire)
43	The Emperor Claudius gives the command to invade Britain
49-50	Caratacus fights back. Roman army starts to take over Wales
51	Caratacus defeated. He is honoured by the Welsh for being a brave leader
56	Druid sanctuary in Anglesey destroyed
60	Queen Boudicca rebels against the Romans
68	Civil war in Rome with four men struggling to become emperor. Vespasian wins - he had been a soldier in Britain
122	Hadrian visits Britain. Hadrian's Wall is built as a frontier to keep the north of England safe from raids
143	Frontier extended into Scotland. Antonine Wall built to hold the Lowlands, in reign of Antoninus Pius. Yorkshire tribe of Brigantes revolt

160s	Antonine Wall abandoned. Frontier goes back to Hadrian's Wall
212	All freedmen made Roman citizens
259-74	Britain becomes part of a breakaway Gallic Empire with France and Germany, ruled by Postumus
270	Carausius given job of getting rid of pirates in the English Channel. Seizes power and becomes ruler of Gaul and Britain
270	Forts on the south coast of England (known as the Saxon Shore) built to fight off Saxon raids
303	Great persecution of Christians
306	Constantine declared emperor at York
313	Freedom of worship for all Christians
314	British bishops go to Council in Arles
367	Picts and Saxons combine to attack Britain. Count Theodosius fights them off and makes Britain safe again
395	Emperor Theodosius dies. Saxons, Picts and Scots attack Britain, defeated by Stilicho
402	Troops leave Britain to go to protect Italy
409	Roman power collapses, British told to look to their own defences
455	Rome pillaged by Vandals

Roman Britain

Felicity Hebditch

Evans Brothers Limited

First published in this edition in 2003 by
Evans Brothers Limited
2A Portman Mansions
Chiltern St
London W1U 6NR

First published in hardback in 1996.
© Evans Brothers Limited 1996

Published in paperback in 1996. Reprinted 1998.

Printed in Belgium

A catalogue record for this book is available from
the British Library.

ISBN 0 237 52636 0

Acknowledgements
Design: Ann Samuel
Editorial: Nicola Barber
Illustrations: Nick Hawken
Production: Jenny Mulvanny

VISIT OUR WEBSITE
www.evansbooks.co.uk
Evans

Acknowledgements

For permission to reproduce copyright material,
the author and publishers gratefully acknowledge
the following:

Cover (main & middle) The Bridgeman Art
Library, (background) Corinium Museum,
Cirencester, (top) Skyscan Balloon
Photography/English Heritage Photo Library,
(bottom) Sonia Halliday Photographs. Title page
Corinium Museum, Cirencester. Contents page
British Museum, London/The Bridgeman Art
Library. page 6 Peter Scholey/Robert Harding
Picture Library. page 7 P.M Origin of London/
Robert Harding Picture Library. page 8 (top)
Giraudon/The Bridgeman Art Library, (bottom)
the art archive page 9 (top) Derek Berwin/The
Image Bank, (bottom) Adam Woolfitt/ Robert
Harding Picture Library. page 10 News Team
International. page 11 (top) National Museum of
Antiquities, Edinburgh/The Bridgeman Art
Library, (bottom) FHC Birch/Sonia Halliday
Photographs p.12 (left) English Heritage
Photographic Library, (right) Ivan Lapper/English
Heritage. page 13 Robert Harding Picture Library.
page 14 (top) Corinium Museum, Cirencester, (bot-
tom) Verulamium Museum, St Albans. page 16
(top) Tyne and Wear County Council Museum,
(bottom) Ghigo Roli/Robert Harding Picture
Library. page 17 (top) Peter Clayton, (bottom)
Victoria and Albert Museum/The Bridgeman Art
Library. page 18 (top) Lauros-Giraudon/ The
Bridgeman Art Library (bottom left and right)
Werner Forman Archive. page 19 Julie
Meech/Ecoscene. page 20 Somerset County
Museum, Taunton Castle/The Bridgeman Art
Library. page 21 (top) Giraudon/The Bridgeman
Art Library. page 22 (bottom left) Michael Holford,
(bottom right) Verulamium Museum, St
Albans/The Bridgeman Art Library. page 23 (top)
Verulamium Museum, St Albans, (middle) British
Museum/Michael Holford, (bottom)
Giraudon/The Bridgeman Art Library. page 24
(top) Roman Baths Museum, Bath/Michael
Holford, (bottom) Museo Nazionale Romano,
Rome/Werner Forman Archive. page 25 (top)
Werner Forman Archive, (bottom) Dorset County
Museum/The Bridgeman Art Library. page 26
(top) Robert Frerck/Robert Harding Picture
Library, (bottom)) Robert
Frerck/Odyssey/Chicago/Robert Harding Picture
Library. page 27 (top) University of Cambridge,
(bottom) British Museum, London/The
Bridgeman Art Library. page 28 the art archive.
page 29 (top) Robert Harding Picture Library, (bot-
tom) University of Cambridge.

CONTENTS

A GREAT CITY AND A LITTLE ISLAND

Rome

Rome began as a little huddle of villages. The Romans dated the foundation of their city to 753 BC. By 30 BC – the time of the first emperor, Augustus – Rome had become a huge city of a million people. This great city was the centre of an empire that covered most of Europe and North Africa. The Roman Empire lasted for more than 400 years. In AD 43, Britain became a part of this mighty empire, a far-away island on the edge of the Roman world.

> *The entire civilised world is ruled by this great city.*
>
> Aelius Aristides writing about Rome in *Orationes xxvi* AD 143

These are the ruins of the main forum, or market place, in Rome. As Rome grew into a great city, the Romans built several market places.

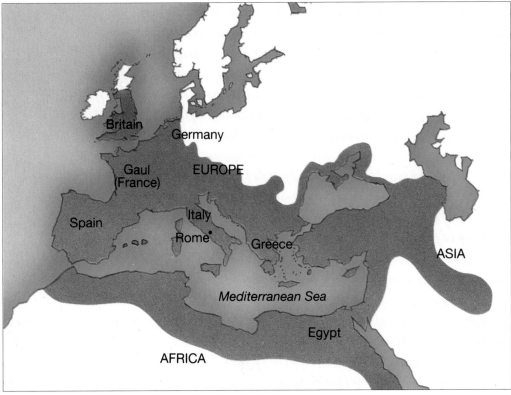

This map shows the Roman Empire in AD 117, when it covered its largest area.

Words, words, words ....

We count our years from when Jesus Christ was born; it will soon be AD 2000 (*Anno Domini* – Year of Our Lord). We call the years before the birth of Jesus Christ BC (Before Christ).

The Romans counted years from when Rome was founded in 753 BC. So for them AD 2000 would have been 2753 AUC (*Ab Urbe Condita* – From the Beginning of the City).

The story of Roman Britain begins with the people who lived in Britain before the Romans arrived. The British were related to the Celtic peoples in Europe, the Germans and the Gauls (in present-day France). They were country people, living in villages or farms, and they spoke languages similar to Welsh and Gaelic. The British were organised into tribes, each tribe ruled by a king. Rival tribes often fought each other for power and for land. Each king had a loyal group of warriors who fought with him. To protect their children and animals during times of war, the British built big forts on the tops of hills surrounded by deep ditches and high wooden walls.

How do we know?

Britain became part of the Roman Empire in AD 43, nearly 2000 years ago. How can we know what happened so long ago?

A lot of what people know about Roman Britain comes from books written by the Romans themselves. There may once have been more books about Britain, but only two survive today. The great Roman general, Julius Caesar, described what he saw in Britain during his invasions in his book *De Bello Gallico (The Gallic Wars)*, and a writer called Tacitus wrote about his wife's father, Agricola, who was governor of Britain from AD 78. (You can find extracts from the writings of Caesar and Tacitus throughout this book.)

Another way of finding out about the past is archaeology – digging up remains from the past and studying them. Through the centuries people have dug up the ruins of Roman buildings, roads and wells, as well as coins, pots, pieces of pottery and many other remains that tell us about life in Roman Britain.

Doing a 'dig' is rather like trying to fit together all the pieces of a jigsaw. As different remains are dug out of the ground, archaeologists label them carefully. They then study each piece to work out how old it is. They also look at the ground where things are found to try to understand exactly what happened at the site, using clues like detectives.

This map shows the names and regions of the Celtic tribes in Britain.

These 'diggers' are finding out how the walls were built around the Roman city of Londinium (London).

Venicones
Damnonii
Epidii
Votadini
Selgovae
Novantae
Brigantes
Parisi
Deceangli
Coritani
Ordovices
Iceni
Cornovii
Trinovantes
Demetae
Dobunni
Catuvellauni
Silures
Atrebates
Cantii
Durotriges
Regnenses
Dumnonii

7

JULIUS CAESAR INVADES BRITAIN

In 59 BC the Roman general, Julius Caesar, was put in charge of an army to conquer the warlike tribes of Gaul (France). As Caesar extended Roman rule across Gaul, the British often came to the help of the Gauls. So Julius Caesar decided to teach the British a lesson. It was he who led a Roman army as it landed for the first time on British shores.

The mighty Roman army

It was the might of the Roman army that made Rome great. The army was well-organised and well-trained. The soldiers belonged to a group called a century, originally 100 men. Each century was led by a centurion. Sixty centuries made a legion of 6000 soldiers in Caesar's army. By the time of Claudius, there were only 80 fighting men in a century, but there were also extra men with special skills, such as engineers.

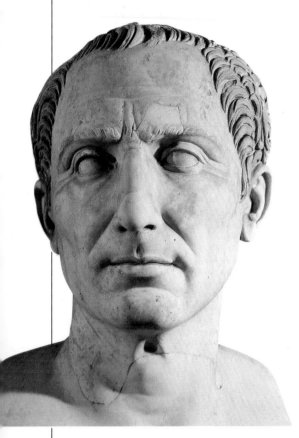

Julius Caesar was a very clever general and he led his soldiers to many victories.

Roman soldiers were expected to do more than just fight. Here they are cutting wood to build a fort.

Before the time of Julius Caesar, only people from Rome could become 'legionaries' – soldiers in the Roman legions. The legionaries were very brave and disciplined. In battle they moved together, following their standard bearer who carried a Roman eagle high in the air. When the legionaries charged, they held their shields overlapping in front of them, like a wall.

As the Roman Empire expanded, soldiers from different parts of the empire came to fight for the Roman army. These recruits were called auxiliaries (which means 'helping' or 'back-up' soldiers). Eventually auxiliaries were allowed to join the legions, and become legionaries too. Many of them were good at riding horses, and they became cavalry troops.

Words, words, words ....

'Century' means 'a hundred' from the Latin word *centum* (hundred). *Decem* (ten) gives us 'decimals'. *Mille* (thousand) gives us 'millennium' as well as 'millipede'.

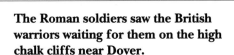

British warriors

In 55 BC, the ships of Julius Caesar's fleet dropped anchor off the coast near modern-day Dover. Above them on the high cliffs the Romans could see the British warriors. In his book, Caesar wrote about the British: 'They dye their skin with woad which makes them blue, and they look more terrifying in battle.' The British were very brave fighters. But the discipline and determination of the Roman legionaries eventually won the battles.

The Roman ships containing food supplies for the army were wrecked, so the soldiers took wheat from the Britons' fields. Caesar wrote that the British had farms with lots of cattle.

The Roman soldiers saw the British warriors waiting for them on the high chalk cliffs near Dover.

> *Veni, vidi, vici*
> (I came, I saw, I conquered)
>
> Julius Caesar writing about his invasions

The Roman army returned to Gaul for the winter. The following year, a British prince from the tribe called the Trinovantes came to Caesar to ask for help fighting against the Catuvellauni. The Catuvellauni was a powerful tribe and its warriors were trying to take over land belonging to other smaller tribes. The Romans agreed and this time Caesar's army captured one of the Catuvellauni's hill-forts and won several battles. But Caesar had to go back to fight more wars in Gaul. He never returned to Britain.

It's true!

There are over a thousand hill-forts in Britain. You can visit most of them and climb round the big ditches dug to defend them.

British warriors had beautiful shields and swords. This shield was found in the River Thames at Battersea in London.

CLAUDIUS CONQUERS BRITAIN

In AD 43 the Emperor Claudius decided to invade Britain. He had heard stories of gold and silver in this far-off island. What's more, he needed a victory abroad to make him more popular at home. When another British prince came to the Romans to complain about the Catuvellauni, this gave Claudius the perfect excuse to make Britain part of the great Roman Empire. Claudius sent an army of 50,000 men. They brought everything they needed to conquer a new country – supplies of food and armour, timber and tents. There were engineers, carpenters, surveyors, people to make armour, even people to repair ships.

This time the British weren't waiting for the Romans on the coast. But the kings of the Catuvellauni, Caratacus and his brother, tried to stop the advancing Roman army from crossing the River Medway in Kent. Imagine wading into the deep, fast-flowing waters of a cold river with frightening blue men throwing spears at you! However, the Romans conquered the British and marched into the British town of Camulodunum (Colchester), the capital of the Catuvellauni. The Emperor Claudius came to join in the triumph – he rode in style with elephants he brought with him!

The Roman army soon controlled all of lowland Britain south of the line of the Fosse Way, a long road from Exeter to Lincoln which still exists. But the mountain areas were more difficult to conquer. The next Roman campaign was in Wales, from about AD 49. After his defeat at Colchester, Caratacus had fled to Wales from where he led many attacks against the Romans. He became a Welsh hero, but he was betrayed by the British queen of the Brigantes in Yorkshire in AD 51.

Words, words, words ....

The Roman army built well-fortified camps wherever they stayed. There are many places called after the Latin word for a 'camp' *castra*, such as **Chester**, Don**caster**, Lei**cester** and Col**chester** in England, and **Caer**went and Y **Gaer** in Wales.

Roman camps had a wall around them and a gateway where a sentry could keep watch. This is the Lunt Roman fort near Coventry.

Rebellion

While much of the Roman army was busy in Wales, a new revolt started in eastern England. In AD 60 Boudicca, queen of the Iceni, started a rebellion against Roman rule. She was angry about the way the Romans had treated her people, and especially about the way the Romans had taken their money and land. Led by their Queen, the Iceni and Trinovantes set Colchester on fire, and Verulamium (St Albans) and Londinium (London) too. But when Boudicca's warriors met the ordered Roman legions, they were defeated. Boudicca's kingdom in East Anglia never recovered from the rebellion. For centuries afterwards, it was a poor region.

> *The people who live in Scotland have red hair. Those in South Wales have swarthy complexions, ...and they are supposed to have come from Spain.*
>
> Tacitus writing in AD 84

A Roman cavalryman in action against the British. This carving comes from the Antonine Wall in Scotland.

Scotland

The tribes of Scotland were even more difficult to subdue than the Welsh. Roman writers often called these fierce people Picts, meaning 'painted people' because they were covered with tattoos. In AD 122 the Emperor Hadrian came to Britain and decided to build a stone wall with forts along it in order to keep the Picts out of England. This wall was named Hadrian's Wall after the emperor.

In the AD 140s the Romans decided to take over Lowland Scotland and they built another wall, the Antonine Wall. This wall crossed the narrowest part of Scotland, from the Firth of Clyde to the Firth of Forth. But supplying enough soldiers to patrol such a huge area was a problem, so after only 20 years the northern frontier changed back to Hadrian's Wall.

Hadrian's Wall was built to keep out the Scots, and stop them attacking farms and towns in the north of England.

BUILDING ROMAN BRITAIN

*A*griciola helped them build temples, town centres and houses

Tacitus writing in AD 84 about his father-in-law, Agricola, who was governor of Britain from AD 78

The Romans were very good at planning and organising people. After invading and conquering Britain, or any foreign country, one of the first things they did was to build roads. These roads helped the Romans to run their empire efficiently because messages and supplies could be taken quickly from place to place, and soldiers could march easily to wherever there was trouble.

Roman soldiers built the roads. First, a surveyor set out the line the road would take, as straight as possible. Then a ditch was dug at each side to drain the road and layers of stones were laid down. Milestones along the road gave the name of the emperor in whose reign the road was made or mended, and the distance from the nearest town. Roman roads were so well-made that they remained the best roads in Britain for more than a thousand years!

This map shows the Roman road network in Britain, and the position of places mentioned in this book.

The ruins of the Roman town of Wroxeter have been uncovered by archaeologists.

This painting shows what Wroxeter looked like in Roman times. Can you see the builders with piles of wood starting to build a new part?

Before the Romans arrived, the British lived in small village settlements. But the Romans thought that town life would make the British want to be good Roman citizens. The first towns in Britain were built for the Roman soldiers to live in. Soon, many British people were changing to a Roman way of life and building Roman-style houses, furniture and the latest fashions.

Whereas British villages followed the shape of the land on which they were built, the Romans laid out their towns in squares with the roads at right angles. In the centre of a town they built a market place or forum, a town hall with law courts or basilica, a temple and shops. On the edge of town, there was a theatre or amphitheatre where spectacular athletic shows, bearfights and plays were held.

The Romans were keen on hygiene. In their towns, they built public baths with hot rooms and an icy cold plunge pool. Every town had a clean water supply, sometimes brought by an aqueduct. The water was taken to houses and shops through wooden or lead pipes. There were public toilets with water and sewers. The dead were buried or cremated in cemeteries outside the town.

Each town was run by a council of local people. There were two magistrates to oversee the law courts, and two to look after public buildings and roads, aqueducts, fountains and sewers.

Words, words, words ....

The word 'street' comes from the Latin word *strata*, meaning 'layers laid down'.

It's true!

The Romans had a postal system for sending official messages and for collecting taxes. The postman travelled on horseback or in a carriage. He could cover 80 kilometres in a day, though it was possible to travel up to 250 kilometres if a message was urgent. Each town had to provide a place for the postman to stay overnight, like a motel, where he could rest, get another horse, and have a meal and a bath.

The city of Bath gets its name from the hot springs which the Romans used to make the Roman baths. You can still visit the baths there.

HOUSES IN ROMAN BRITAIN

Before the arrival of the Romans, British houses were built out of wood or stone and covered with thatch. There were no windows, and a fire burned in the centre of the house, filling the whole house with smoke (see pictures on page 18).

The Romans built their houses out of bricks and tiles, although they used wood as well. The houses of wealthy people had windows with glass in them. Floors were often decorated with mosaics, squares of different colours set in concrete to make patterns or pictures. The walls were covered with plaster and had pictures or patterns painted on them. Many houses had central heating, with a fire made under the concrete floors of some of the rooms, and hollow tiles up the walls to take the warm air round the rooms.

The Romans didn't have carpets on their floors. Instead they often covered floors with mosaics, hundreds of little squares of stone and pottery arranged in a pattern and set into concrete. Parts of this mosaic from Corinium (Cirencester), Gloucestershire, have been destroyed by people digging holes through the earth where it was hidden.

Fishbourne Palace

The first large house in Britain was Fishbourne Palace, near Chichester, Hampshire. It was built for a British prince who was friendly to the Romans. Stone for important buildings was transported by ship all round Britain, and Fishbourne was built out of stone brought from Gloucestershire, from Purbeck in Dorset and from Caen in France. Fishbourne has a garden in the courtyard which archaeologists have patiently uncovered. In Italy, the Romans had pretty gardens with trellises and statues. Gardens in Britain probably had more vegetables than flowers.

The Romans had a fashion for painting pictures on their walls, or even on ceilings, like this painting of birds from Verulamium (St Albans), Hertfordshire.

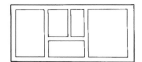

The first houses were quite simple.

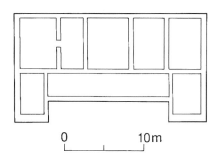

0   10m

Some of these houses were extended by adding rooms, sometimes a corridor and 'wings' (extra rooms at each end).

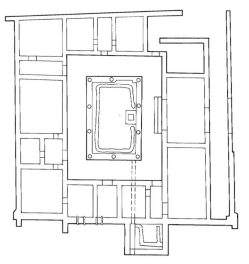

Sometimes there was a courtyard with rooms all round. Some of the rooms in a house were used for business, like an office. Part of a room could be divided off with a curtain to make a bedroom.

Although the walls of most Roman houses in Britain have been destroyed, you can often still make out where they stood. Sometimes the shape of the walls show up in photographs taken from an aeroplane. By digging at sites where there was a Roman house, archaeologists have found out how many rooms there were, and their size.

Between AD 100 and 300, rich British families built big houses in the towns. But from AD 300 to 400 more big villas or houses were built in the countryside than in the towns. Perhaps the people who built these country houses were trying to avoid paying taxes, which were higher in the towns. Or they might have been escaping from the dangers of the plague which was passed on more easily in the crowded conditions of a town.

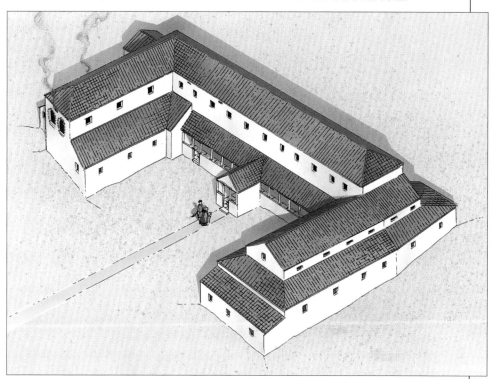

A typical Roman-British villa with 'wings' at either end. The roof is tiled, and the walls are made from stone. Only parts of the house would have had central heating – probably the bathrooms and the dining room.

They began to have... saunas and dinner parties. The Britons called it civilisation when it was just a way of making them Rome's slaves.

Tacitus writing about the British adoption of Roman ways of life.

Words, words, words ....

'Domestic' comes from *domus,* Latin for 'home'.

THE HOUSEHOLD

Family life

A typical family in Roman Britain included father, mother, children and slaves. *Pater* (father) was a Roman citizen. This meant that he had the right to trade, to marry, and to hold office as a magistrate or government worker. In AD 212 all men in the Roman Empire who weren't slaves were made Roman citizens.

Pater ruled over his household. In Roman law women didn't have any rights, and husbands could divorce their wives (*mater:* mother). Children (*filius:* son and *filia:* daughter) weren't much better off. Their father could beat them if he wanted to.

People became slaves (*servus:* slave) after being captured in war, or sometimes kidnapped and sold. Slaves belonged to their master or mistress and they had to obey their owners' orders. Some slaves were treated badly – they were kept in chains or poorly fed. Other slaves became part of the family. Slaves could earn their freedom with good work, or they could be freed by their owners. They were then known as freedmen or freedwomen.

Regina the slave

A dealer called Barates from Palmyra in Syria worked in Britain selling military standards. He had a slave called Regina who was from the Catuvellauni tribe. He made her free and married her. Her tombstone from South Shields, Tyneside, is written in two languages: Latin and Palmyran.

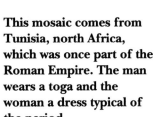

What did they wear?

The most famous piece of Roman clothing is the toga, but in fact, only Roman citizens were allowed to wear togas! They were usually for formal occasions. At other times, a man in Roman Britain wore a cloak over a simple tunic, or one tunic over another. Women wore a long dress pinned with brooches. Brooches were easy to lose, and archaeologists often find them in excavations. Boys wore a tunic, like a long tee-shirt. Girls wore dresses, like their mothers.

Roman soldiers on duty in northern Britain needed warmer clothes than those normally worn in sunny Italy. Here is part of a letter found at Vindolanda, a fort on Hadrian's Wall:

I have sent you ...pairs of socks, two pairs of sandals, two pairs of underpants...

This mosaic comes from Tunisia, north Africa, which was once part of the Roman Empire. The man wears a toga and the woman a dress typical of the period.

In the dining room

The Romans had a good, healthy diet. In the summer there was plenty of fresh food, but in the winter there were not many fruits or vegetables. There were no greenhouses, and people couldn't keep food in freezers or tins as we do today. So most of the food for winter was dried or salted to preserve it, and it was very dull.

A Roman dining room had couches on which to lie, little tables with glassware and pottery, and oil lamps. The walls were painted with pictures, and mosaics made the floor attractive and easy to clean. Some Britons preferred to have a hall (like a barn) where they could invite a lot of people to a feast.

The British way of cooking was over a wood fire. The Romans had charcoal barbecue-type stoves. It is likely that both methods were used in Britain.

The Romans relaxed on couches, like beds, to eat their meals. This man is being served by a little boy who is probably his slave.

A Roman recipe

4 eggs
100 grams pine kernels
$\frac{1}{2}$ teaspoon lovage
$\frac{1}{2}$ teaspoon honey
$1\frac{1}{2}$ tablespoons white wine vinegar
1 teaspoon garum *
black pepper

Ask an adult to help you.
Put eggs in boiling water and simmer for 5 minutes. Plunge into cold water, leave for 8 minutes and peel. Liquidize the pine kernels or pound them in a mortar until they are like thick cream, then put into a bowl with the lovage, honey, vinegar, garum and plenty of black pepper. Stir, and pour over the eggs.

* This was a fish sauce the Romans loved; you can use anchovy essence.

A glass jug and a bottle. The Romans were very good at making glass objects.

IN THE COUNTRYSIDE

When the Romans arrived, much of Britain was covered with small farms. The British grew wheat for bread, and barley to make beer. Wheat was very important to the Romans because the army needed regular supplies. Ships took wheat all over the empire for the army. To make more land for growing crops, Roman engineers improved boggy areas like the Fenlands in East Anglia by draining them.

The army was always anxious to have enough food to feed all its soldiers – there might be a riot if the troops didn't have good rations! Here is part of a letter found at the fort at Vindolanda, Hadrian's Wall:

I have bought about 5000 modii of grain so I need some cash for it. Send me some cash as soon as possible...

These people are picking fruit on a Roman farm. The Romans knew how to prune trees, and they brought new kinds of fruit to Britain.

Fruit and vegetables

Market gardening improved once there were towns with markets where people went to shop regularly. The Romans brought new plants to Britain such as grapes, cherries, mulberries, celery, marrows and radishes. They grew better varieties of apples and pears, and vegetables such as onions and peas. They also introduced useful new plants such as hemp – used to make ropes, and flax – used to make linen.

Archaeologists at Little Butser farm in Hampshire have experimented with ways of building the kinds of houses in which the British people lived before the arrival of the Romans.

Animals

British farmers raised cattle, sheep and pigs, but the Romans brought bigger and better breeds, such as sheep with softer wool. The Romans showed the British how to make hay to feed animals in the winter.

The British kept good hunting dogs and these were sold abroad. But the Romans brought with them little pet dogs and cats too. We know all this because archaeologists can identify animals when they find their bones. They have also found the footprints of cats and dogs on tiles, made as the animals walked on the tiles when the clay was soft.

> *They do not think it right to eat hares or chickens or geese but they keep them for interest and for fun.*
>
> Julius Caesar writing about the British in *De Bello Gallico V 12-14*

Words, words, words ....

'Mill' comes from the Latin *molina*. Most mills were turned by hand or by a donkey, but the Romans also built water mills, where the power of running water was used to turn the wheels to grind corn.

It's true!

The Romans didn't invent many machines as they had slaves to do much of their hard work!

Woods

There were some forests with very large trees in Roman Britain, but most were 'managed' woods where the trees were coppiced (cut so that a lot of thin trees grow from the main tree). The Roman docks in London were made of huge pieces of timber from large trees, but the amphitheatre at Silchester, near Reading, was constructed from thin poles taken from coppiced woods.

It's true!

Global warming has happened before! From AD 250 - 400 it was hotter than it is now. We can tell what the weather was like at different times from various clues such as tree rings and pollen. When you cut down a tree, you can see the rings of growth it makes each year, with wide rings for wet summers and narrow rings for dry summers. Archaeologists have built up a pattern of the weather from this evidence.

Plants release tiny grains of pollen. These pollen grains are very tough and last for hundreds of years in the soil. When archaeologists look at the grains through a microscope they can tell which plants the grains came from. Some plants like hot weather and some like a wet climate, so if there are a lot of dry-loving plant pollens, archaeologists know that the weather was dry at a particular time.

Coppiced woods are cut back so that many thin trunks grow from the root of the tree.

BUYING AND SELLING

The Romans were keen businessmen. They bought and sold goods from all over the empire. Roman wrecks have been found with olive oil and fish sauce from Spain, wine in amphorae (jars) from Gaul (France), fine pottery and glass, and wine in barrels from Germany. Smaller loads, such as cloth, came with these goods.

What did Britain sell to other countries?

Minerals – gold, silver, lead and iron – were what the Romans hoped to find in Britain. In fact, there was very little gold, but there is a Roman gold mine at Dolaucothi in Wales. Lead was mined in the Mendips in Somerset and in Derbyshire. A Roman wreck has been found which was carrying British lead for export abroad. Iron was made in the wooded places like the Weald in Kent and the Forest of Dean in Gloucestershire because wood was needed to heat the rock in order to extract the iron (called smelting).

The British made good-quality wool, and exported rugs and a type of cloak with a hood, called a *birrus Britannicus.*

The island produces corn, cattle, gold, silver and iron. All these are exported together with animal skins, slaves, and dogs which are useful for hunting.

Strabo, a Greek geographer, writing before the Romans came to Britain

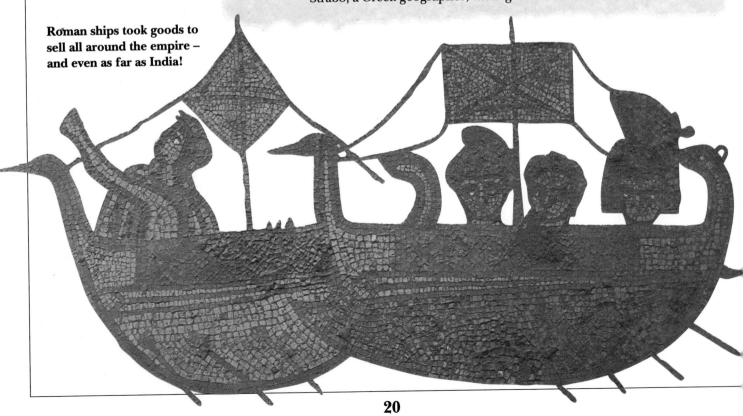

Roman ships took goods to sell all around the empire – and even as far as India!

Shops

In every town there were shops selling everything from bread to cushions, from saucepans to statues of goddesses. Shops were built in rows, with open fronts. Behind each shop was a room where the owner and his family lived. At night the shop was closed with shutters. There were food shops, such as bakers', but as food rots quickly in the ground it is difficult to tell exactly what was sold in these shops. However, archaeologists do find bones from butcher's shops. Cloth from a draper's rots away, but sometimes shoes and leather survive from a cobbler's and the leatherworking tools too. Every town also had shops selling pottery, glass, cutlery and tools.

A Roman butcher's shop. The butcher has some scales (on the right) to weigh the meat.

Coins

Some Celtic tribes made their own coins by copying Greek designs.

Roman money was used all over the empire and in countries beyond. The money was brought from mints in Gaul (France) and Germany to pay the soldiers. The soldiers wouldn't use Celtic money. On one side of a Roman coin was the head of the emperor with his name, and on the other side was a picture to show countries he had conquered.

A British coin (left), made from gold, showing Cunobelinus the king of the Catuvellauni. The Roman coin (right) shows the Emperor Hadrian. It says:

IMP	CAESAR	TRAIAN	HADRIANUS	AUG
IMPERATOR	CAESAR	TRAIANUS	HADRIANUS	AUGUSTUS
EMPEROR	CAESAR	TRAJAN	HADRIAN	THE MIGHTY

READING AND WRITING

People in Britain spoke Celtic languages like Welsh. The Roman army and government officers spoke Latin. So in order to buy and sell to the Romans, and to learn what was the law, many British people learned Latin. It wasn't just rich people who could write and speak Latin. Some museums have pots on which workmen have scratched words such as: *Bibe*, 'Drink'. And on a tile from the Roman town of Silchester near Reading there are some words from a famous Latin poem, scratched on to the tile by the worker who made it.

Children in Roman Britain were mostly taught by their parents. There were schools for boys in Rome, but we don't know if there were any in Britain. The Romans learned a lot from the Greeks, such as medicine and maths. But not many people in Britain would have been able to speak or write Greek.

Paper, wood and cloth usually rot away in the ground, but they sometimes survive in very dry or very wet places. Letters written on paper in Latin have been found in Egypt. Several letters have also been found in a wet part of the Roman fort of Vindolanda at Hadrian's Wall, written in ink on thin shavings of wood. The ink was made of soot and gum arabic.

You will often see Roman inscriptions (writing) on the remains of arches or tombs. Inscriptions were carved in capital letters. Normally, the Romans wrote letters in a kind of joined-up writing.

It's true!

Sometimes the Romans wrote on wax that had been melted on to wood; two of these tablets could be tied together to keep the writing from being rubbed out.

Two wax tablets, and the metal pen, or stylus, used to scratch words on to the wax.

LIFE AT LEISURE

There were many festivals in the Roman calendar, often celebrating one of the Roman gods. At these festivals, there would be processions, feasting and sports. Each town council organised the celebrations in the amphitheatre. There were boxing matches and bull-fights. Sometimes there were funny plays with actors fooling around – falling over and dropping buckets of water, just like modern-day clowns.

Gladiator fighting was a popular attraction at a Roman festival.

Music

We don't know exactly what Roman music sounded like, but the Romans had bone whistles, trumpets and horns, drums, and lyres like small harps. And of course, they sang songs. There were many popular tunes which an audience in the theatre would recognise after only a few notes.

Games

The Romans played board games, such as draughts or Nine Men's Morris, with pieces made of glass and dice carved out of bone. They may also have played tiddlywinks! Soldiers who had money to spare liked gambling with dice.

Learning to play the lyre (like a small harp). People played the lyre to accompany singing, like the guitar today.

Hunting

Lots of pictures show people hunting with their dogs and spears, bows and arrows. The Romans brought pheasants to Britain, and they also hunted deer, hares, wild boar and ducks. At that time, there were bears and wolves in Britain too!

Counters and dice from a Roman game

Words, words, words ....

The names of the months come from Roman gods and people:
January Janus was the god of gateways and beginnings; he had two faces, one looking back and the other forwards.
February was called after a festival for purifying from fevers: *febris* is the Latin for 'fever'.
March was for Mars, the god of war.
April was the month of buds opening: *aperire* is 'to open'.
May was Maia, the mother goddess who made things grow.
June was Juno, the mother of the gods and wife of Jove or Jupiter.
September was originally the seventh month: *septem* is 'seven'.
October was originally the eighth month: *octo* is 'eight'.
November was the ninth: *novem* is 'nine'.
December was the tenth: *decem* is 'ten'.
Two months were added – **July** in honour of Julius Caesar;
August in honour of Augustus.

RELIGION

Celtic gods

The Celtic people believed in gods and spirits of nature, such as gods of the sky and the sun. Celtic holy men were called druids. The druids made sacrifices and had secret knowledge which they passed on to each other, but never wrote down. They were skilled at healing with plants and herbs. The druids fled to North Wales to escape the Roman invaders. But the Roman army wiped out the Ordovices tribe in Wales, and destroyed the druids' last shrine on the island of Anglesey in AD 60.

Roman religion

The Romans had a whole family of gods, and you can read stories about many of their gods and heroes. Jupiter (or Jove) was the god of the sky and weather, and Juno was his wife. Their children included Mars, god of war; Venus, goddess of love; Diana, goddess of hunting; Pluto, god of the dead; and Mercury god of journeys, trade and healing. There were many other gods and goddesses.

In Britain, the Romans often built temples where there was already a British shrine because the Romans were superstitious and thought these other gods would bring them luck. As a result, the Roman and the Celtic gods became mixed together. The Romans also made their emperors into gods and expected people to worship them. This was one way of making soldiers and people from all over the empire loyal to Rome.

The soldiers in the Roman army brought all sorts of religions with them from their different countries. Some believed in Mithras, a god of light, whom they worshipped in secret ceremonies. Soldiers from Greece and Egypt worshipped the Egyptian goddess of love and beauty, Isis. Some were Christians.

The British god of the Roman baths at Bath was Sul, a god of healing. The Romans called him Sul-Minerva as Minerva was a Roman god of healing. Can you see his flowing, watery locks of hair?

Mithras was a god of light who fought against evil. Here, he is fighting a bull.

In every Roman house there was a small shrine for the spirits of the family's ancestors or gods of the house. Sometimes the family had statues of the gods that they wanted to protect them, such as Venus or Mercury, or sometimes they chose the Celtic god or goddess of the place they lived in.

Christianity

Soldiers of the Roman army who came to Britain between AD 200 and 300 were probably the first to bring Christianity to British shores. At first, Christians had to have services in secret because they were persecuted by the Romans for refusing to worship Roman gods. The Romans thought that Christians made the gods angry and brought bad luck. St Alban was the first Christian martyr we know of in Britain. He lived at a time when Christians were persecuted. He was put to death on the hill outside Verulamium (modern-day St Albans) and the place where he died became a shrine for pilgrims.

In AD 312, the Emperor Constantine became a Christian so he made Christianity the religion of the whole Roman Empire.

A house-shrine from Pompeii in Italy. The father of the family said prayers here, and the family brought gifts such as flowers, fruit or wine.

One of the earliest pictures of Christ in Britain, from a mosaic floor at Hinton St Mary in Dorset.

Words, words, words ....

The Romans liked word puzzles. This one may have been a secret sign between Christians when they were persecuted. It has been found at a number of places, including Cirencester in Gloucestershire:

```
S A T O R
A R E P O
T E N E T
O P E R A
R O T A S
```

It's the same whichever way up you read it. The letters make up the word PATER NOSTER ('Our Father') plus A and O, the beginning and the end of the Greek alphabet.

25

THE END OF ROME

The head of a statue of Constantine from Rome. This head came from a huge statue of the emperor.

It's true!

Constantine's city of Constantinople remained an important city. In 1453 the Turkish army took it over. Today it is called Istanbul.

There are parts of Roman history where we only have bits of information – stories about distant bands of warriors or bags of coins buried in the ground – and we have to guess what was really going on. From the clues that they have, archaeologists and historians have pieced together parts of the jigsaw to give us a picture of the end of the Roman Empire.

One of the main problems was the cost of running the empire. The price of goods kept on going up. Between AD 100 and 200 a measure of corn cost half a denarius; in AD 301 it had gone up to 100 denarii. The cost of keeping such a huge and well-equipped army was enormous, so taxes were also very high.

Another problem was the power of the army. Of course, the army had to be powerful to win wars. But if the soldiers decided to rebel, there was nothing to stop them. From 52 to 46 BC, Julius Caesar used parts of the Roman army loyal to him to make himself dictator in Rome. In AD 196 Albinus took the Roman army away from Britain to make himself emperor. Back in Britain there was chaos as tribes rebelled and burned down Roman forts.

For these and many other reasons, it was difficult to keep the empire together. For a while, from AD 259-74, Britain became part of a break-away mini-empire which included Britain, Gaul (France), Germany and Spain. Then a soldier called Carausius was given the job of getting rid of pirates in the English Channel, but he used his power to make himself ruler of Britain (AD 287-96).

The emperor Diocletian tried to solve the problems of wars in the empire by creating another emperor to work with, so that one could control the eastern part of the empire and one the western part. But after Diocletian retired, the son of one of the new emperors decided to seize power for himself. His name was Constantine. He built a new capital city in the east at Constantinople.

A view over modern-day Istanbul (Constantinople)

The barbarians

All through Roman history the people who lived beyond the frontiers of the Roman Empire, the barbarians, made raids on the towns and countryside. Around AD 250 barbarians destroyed large areas of Gaul and Germany. Britain was quite peaceful, but nevertheless walls were built around many towns to protect them. From about 270 the Romans built forts along the south coast of England (known as the Saxon Shore), where the Saxons from Germany were landing to steal what they could.

Portchester was one of the forts built to defend the south coast of England against the Saxons.

In 367 several barbarian tribes joined together, and Britain was attacked by the Picts from Scotland, the Scotti from Ireland and the Saxons in the south. When Count Theodosius was sent to restore order he found bands of barbarians roaming the land, loaded with loot. In 402 the Roman army that remained in Britain was forced to return to Italy to fight the huge barbarian armies that were attacking. In 410 the Goths looted Rome, and in 455 it was the Vandals' turn. They took all the treasures and destroyed what they couldn't carry. You can see where we get the word 'vandal' from!

A silver Roman dish from Mildenhall in Suffolk. It is part of a treasure hoard found by a farmer while he was ploughing.

Words, words, words ....

'Barbarian' is a word invented by the Greeks. They thought the only civilised language was Greek and everybody else just said "bar bar bar...!"

THE LEGACY OF ROME

Britain after the Romans

Even after the Roman army had left, Britain continued to be Roman in many ways. But without proper defences it was difficult to fight off invaders. Eventually, the Saxons began to settle in the south and the Angles in the east. The area in the west remained more Roman, and in the southwest a king called Arthur ruled. But by the 500s AD, Britain was no longer Roman, and England was the land of the Angles and Saxons. However, the Romans left a rich legacy in all the lands that were once part of their great empire.

Words, words, words ....

There is a large legacy of words in English that come from Latin. Here are some 'body' words:

caput head – 'capital'
oculi eyes – 'oculist'
aures ears – 'aural'
dentes teeth – 'dentist'
bracchia arms – 'bracelet'
manus hand – 'manual'
pedes feet – 'pedal', 'pedestrian'

The legacy of language

Many languages come from Latin, such as French, Spanish, Italian and Romanian. Other languages, such as English and Welsh, have a lot of words from Latin. Latin went on being read, written and spoken for centuries after the Roman Empire ended. The Christian Church used Latin as a language that everyone could speak to each other, whatever country they came from. Even today, plants and animals are given proper names in Latin so that all countries can agree on the correct name.

> *R*oman, it is your special genius to rule the peoples, to impose the ways of peace.
> Virgil (70-19 BC) *Aeneid I*

The Latin name for foxglove is *digitalis*, meaning that it fits on your finger (*digit* means 'finger'). Different countries have their own names for plants, but they all agree to use the standard Latin name as well.

Digitalis purpurea

Words, words, words ....

Caesar's family became the emperors of Rome and his name came to mean 'emperor'. The German word *kaiser* and the Russian word *czar* both come from 'caesar'.

Roman culture and religion

After the break-up of the Roman Empire, the barbarians spread over the areas once controlled by the Romans. The Franks changed Gaul's name to France, the Huns went to Hungary, Goths, Visigoths and Vandals finally settled down and took up where the Romans left off. Today, much of Europe still has Roman law – although in Britain our legal system comes from Saxon law.

The Christian Church continued to link Britain with the rest of Europe. In the Celtic west, Ireland, Cornwall and Wales, Christians kept the faith alive. But in England, the Saxons brought their own gods, and the British began to worship them. In 597 St Augustine was sent by the Pope to teach the Saxons about Christianity and bring the Church back together. St Augustine became the first Archbishop of Canterbury.

People in many countries have copied the Roman idea of a grand archway. This is Marble Arch in London. It's rather like the Roman archway on page 22.

Taken from the air, this photo shows just how straight some Roman roads were!

The legacy of the land

Counties in Britain are still roughly based on the territories of the various British tribes. The Roman towns that ruled these tribes continue to be important towns for their area – for example, York, Lincoln, Gloucester, Winchester, Chester and many others. The roads that the Romans made were the only proper roads until the 18th century, and Watling Street, Stane Street and many others form the routes of our roads today. Look at maps of Britain and you will often see the words **Roman Road** marked along a remarkably straight road!

There are a few big Roman buildings still standing, such as the gateway at Lincoln, the Roman baths at Bath, and the Roman town walls at York, London or Caerwent in Wales.

Tempus fugit
(Time flies)

Virgil (70-19 BC) *Georgics III*

Vale! (Goodbye!)

Index

Glossary

amphitheatre   a circular stadium with seats, like a football stadium

amphora   a big pottery jar with two handles, to hold wine, oil etc.

aqueduct   a big pipe or channel to carry water

archaeology   the scientific study of ancient things

basilica   a large hall used for the law courts and town hall

Celts   the ancient people of western Europe

couch   a seat to lie on at a meal, like a settee

cremated   burned

denarius   a Roman coin

druids   Celtic priests

excavation   a 'dig' done by archaeologists

forum   market place

freedmen/freedwomen   slaves set free

frontier   the border or edge of a country

Gaul   the Roman name for France

inscription   something written on a tomb, archway, pot etc.

legion   1000 soldiers in the Roman army

magistrate   an officer in charge of running a town and the law

martyr   somebody put to death for their beliefs

mosaic   a picture made up of little coloured squares of stone

Picts   one of the Scottish tribes

plague   a serious disease

Roman citizen   a member of the Roman state with Roman rights

slave   a servant belonging to a person and not free

villa   a Roman house

woad   a plant that makes a blue dye

Places to visit

Museums

British Museum, Great Russell St, London, WC1B 3DG.
Tel: 0171 636 1555

Castle Museum, Colchester, Essex, COI ITJ. Tel: 01206 712288

City and County Museum, Broadgate, Lincoln, LN2 1HQ.
Tel: 01522 30401

City Museum and Art Gallery, Brunswick Road, Gloucester,
GL1 1HP. Tel: 01452 524131

Corinium Museum, Park St, Cirencester, Glos., GL7 1BR.
Tel: 01258 655611

Dorset County Museum, Dorchester, Dorset, DT1 1XA.
Tel: 01305 262735

Dover Museum, Market Square, Dover, Kent, CT16 1PB.
Tel: 01304 201066

Hull and East Riding Museum, 36 High St, Hull.
Tel: 01482 593902

Jewry Wall Museum of Archaeology, St Nicholas Circle,
Leicester, LE5 ORD. Tel: 01533473021

Lancaster City Museum, Market Square, Lancaster, LA1 1HT.
Tel: 01524 64637

Lunt Roman Fort, Baginton, nr Coventry. Tel: 01203 303567

**Museum of Antiquities of the University and the Society of
Antiquaries of Newcastle upon Tyne**, The University,
Newcastle upon Tyne, NE1 7RU. Tel: 0191 222 6000

Museum of London, London Wall, EC2Y 5HN.
Tel: 0171 600 3699

Roman Baths Museum, Pump Room, Stall St, Bath, Avon, BA1
1LZ. Tel: 01225 461111

Roman Legionary Museum, High St, Caerleon, Gwent,
NP6 1AE. Tel: 01633 423134

Roman Museum, Butchery Lane, Canterbury, Kent, CT1 2JE.
Tel: 01227 452747

Roman Town and Museum, Main St, Boroughbridge,
North Yorks, YO2 3PH. Tel: 01423 322768

Tullie House Museum and Art Gallery, Carlisle, Cumbria,
CA3 8TP. Tel: 01228 34781

Verulamium Museum, St Albans, Herts, AL3 4SW.
Tel: 01727 819339

Roman army

Chesters Roman Fort, Corbridge Roman Site Manager,
Corbridge, Northumberland, NE45 5NT.
Tel: 01434 681379

Roman villas

Bignor Roman Villa, Bignor, Pulborough, West Sussex,
RH20 1PH. Tel: 01798 869259

Chedworth Roman Villa, Chedworth, Glos. (National Trust)
Tel: 01242 890256

Fishbourne Roman Palace, Salthill Road, Fishbourne,
nr Chichester, West Sussex, PO19 3QR. Tel: 01243 785859

Rockbourne Roman Villa, under care of Hampshire County
Museum Service, Chilcomb House, Chilcomb Lane,
Winchester, Hants, SO23 8RD. Tel: 01962 846304

Roman Villa, Brading, Isle of Wight. Tel: 01983 406223

Welwyn Roman Baths, under the care of Mill Green Museum,
Mill Green, Hatfield, Herts, AL9 5PD. Tel 01707 271362

Sites

Dover Roman Lighthouse, inside Dover Castle. Tel: 01304
201628/211067

Portchester Castle, near Portsmouth. (English Heritage) Tel:
01705 378291

Silchester, near Reading, Berks. Site signposted from village.
Finds in Reading Museum.

Iron age

Andover Museum and Museum of the Iron Age, 6 Church
Close, Andover, Hants, SP10 1DP. Tel: 01264 366283 and
visit Danebury Hillfort nearby